Witness to WAR

Frontispiece. Ruth Macnair (1899–1986), the author of the letters.

Witness to WAR

*The letters, paintings and photographs of a
Naval officer's wife from Gibraltar July–August 1936*

RUTH MACNAIR

EDITED BY MILES MACNAIR

BREWIN BOOKS

First published by
Brewin Books Ltd, 56 Alcester Road,
Studley, Warwickshire B80 7LG in 2007
www.brewinbooks.com

© Miles Macnair 2007

All rights reserved.

ISBN: 978 1 85858 407 2

The moral right of the author has been asserted.

A Cataloguing in Publication Record
for this title is available from the British Library.

Typeset in Baskerville
Printed in Great Britain by
Warwick Printing Ltd.

Contents

Introduction — 1

Historical Background — 5

Witness To War — 11

Epilogue — 41

HMS Shamrock at Sea.

Introduction

My parents' marriage was a true love-affair, one that lasted for 62 years. My mother was an only child, the daughter of Capt. Edgar Dent of the Kings Own Scottish Borderers and May Sellar, a granddaughter of Patrick Sellar, the controversial 'factor' to the Duke of Sutherland during the early Highland clearances at the start of the 19th century.

In 1916, Ruth Dent was 17 and staying with her great aunt in Edinburgh; her father had died ten years earlier from illness contracted in his military campaigns in the Sudan and South Africa. She had been educated largely by a succession of governesses, and was, at the time she met my father, studying at the Edinburgh Art School. (She became an accomplished painter in watercolours and pastels, a talent that gave her enormous pleasure throughout her life and left a charming legacy to her children). My father, Ian Macnair, was four years older and destined for a career in the Royal Navy from childhood. He was the second son of John Frederick 'Jack' Macnair and Veronica Evans-Pugh. The Macnairs came from Ayrshire and Jack Macnair spent most of his life in India, as a partner in one of the great trading companies in Calcutta. It was in Calcutta that he met and married Veronica Evans-Pugh, granddaughter of the leading Indigo planter in Bengal, James Hills, and daughter of Lewis Evans-Pugh, a barrister who served on the Viceroy's council and who later became MP for Aberystwith. Veronica's sister Evelyn had married another of Patrick Sellar's grandchildren, and it was this mutual relationship that led to my parents' first introduction. Father recalled it in a poem he wrote on their 16th wedding anniversary, when he was at sea and they were separated by the demands of duty.

'You stole my heart on an Edinburgh stair;
And there's a tale begun!
But oh my love, it is hardly fair,
Whenever a day we cannot share,
To take the sparkle out of the air
And the splendour out of the sun.'

Father had fought as a midshipman on the battle-cruiser HMS Inflexible at the Battle of the Falkland Islands in December 1914 and later at Jutland. He had recently returned from the debacle in the Dardenelles when he rode over from Queensferry on his much prized motorcycle, 'Boanerges' (one of the 'Sons of Thunder') for tea with his cousin. It was love at first sight, but any question of an early engagement was frustrated by the rule that marriage allowance was not paid to officers under the age of 25. Father was by no means well off – his own father had died in 1908 and his mother would remain a widow for another 62 years. His solution was immediately to volunteer for the submarine service – an extra 3 shillings and 4 pence per day – and he would continue in this hazardous profession until 1930. His first posting was to one of Admiral Fisher's ambitious steam submarines, the 'K' boats, and it was only because he was ashore with mumps that he missed being drowned at the 'Battle of May Island'; that intensely embarrassing and fatal exercise off the Firth of Forth in February 1918.

My parents were married from May Dent's house in the New Forest on August 7, 1918, and for the next 30 years my mother would 'follow the fleet' wherever and whenever it was possible. There were postings to Hong Kong and Wei-Hai-Wei in 1920/1 and 1927, during which she corresponded frequently with her own mother back in England and these letters, vividly describing the life of a naval wife on station, have already been published. *('China Wife' edited by Eleanor Macnair, Falcon Books 1999)*. They capture the routine and the monotony; the flashes of excitement when emergencies arise; the picnics, the bathing parties and the dances; the golf and the cricket matches; the long voyages out and back on trooping liners, and the companionship of other ward-room wives. And they are illustrated with Ruth Macnair's lively watercolours of a world that has long-since disappeared.

By the early 30s, Ian Macnair was serving in destroyers, with a spell in home waters and another in Malta. 1935/6 found them in Gibraltar, with my father in command of the Defence Flotilla from the bridge of HMS Shamrock. They had married quarters up on the Rock and it was from there that Mother recommenced her correspondence back to the New Forest. The Spanish Civil War was about to explode around her and she had a grandstand seat, admittedly on the sidelines, for the start of the first 'modern' war of the 20th century. As Laurie Lee recalled in his autobiography "As I walked out one midsummer morning";

'It started in the middle of July. There were no announcements, no newspapers, just a whispering in the street and the sound of a woman weeping.'

Miles Macnair 2007.

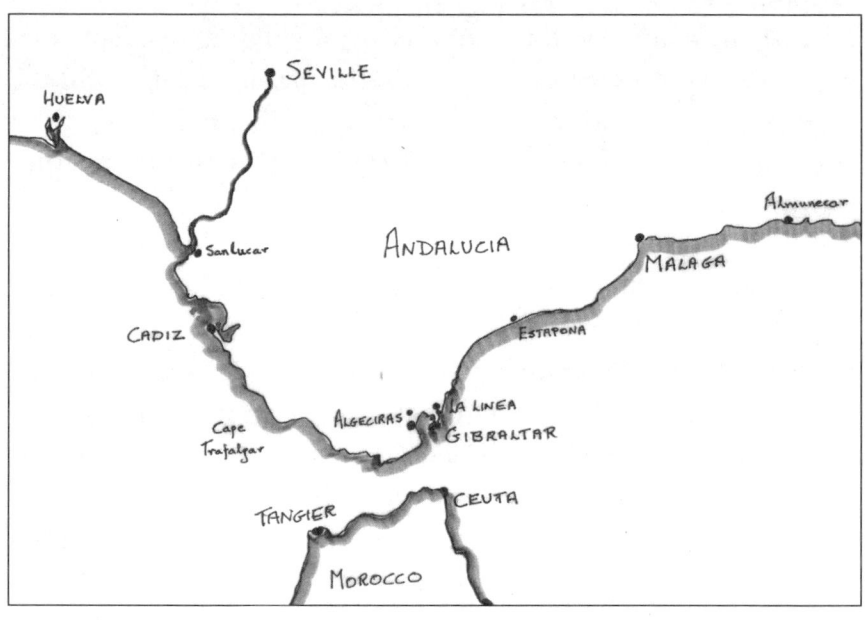

Map of the region around Gibraltar showing the key places mentioned in Ruth's letters.

Historical Background

The origins of the Spanish Civil War can be traced far back in the history of the country, even to the re-conquest from the Moors in 1492 by Queen Isabella of Castille and her consort Ferdinand of Aragon. This liberation would, on the one hand, be revered as a triumph of Catholic supremacy over 'infidels', yet on the other would lead to the suppression of liberal tolerance that had flourished under the Khalifs of Granada. The seat of power would be Madrid, aspirations for any form of regional autonomy would be suppressed and religious toleration extinguished by the Inquisition. There would later be a brief period of Imperial power and the 'glorious' conquests in the Americas, with treasure ships returning full of gold that would adorn the churches but do nothing to enhance the wealth of the nation overall. The pattern of a feudal aristocracy owning all the land and controlling a peasant population in serfdom had been reinforced.

The Roman Catholic Church exerted a huge influence on the lives of all Spaniards and it played a powerful role in politics at every level. Its condemnation of usury in all its aspects, including sound, commercial banking, meant that Spain did not spawn a middle class of merchants and traders like England and the Netherlands in the 17th and 18th centuries. There was a brief flowering of 'liberalism' during the Napoleonic occupation of the country in the first decade of the 19th century, a realisation that the yoke of an oppressor (in this case a foreign one) could be broken by a popular uprising – but only as the junior partner of another foreign force, the army of Great

Britain under the Duke of Wellington. Protagonists on both sides of the Civil War of 1936–39 would hear echoes of this conflict as a crucial precedent.

The defeat of Napoleon resulted in the Constitution of Madrid in 1812, under which several provinces tried to set themselves up as self-governing units within a national federation. But this movement was crushed by Ferdinand VII in 1823 – with the 'invited' assistance of a large army sent by Louis XVIII of France. When Ferdinand died in 1833, two distinct factions within the Spanish army supported rival claimants to the throne; his daughter, who became Queen Isabella II, and his brother Don Carlos. This resulted in the 'first' civil war of 1833–40, and rivalry between the Bourbon Monarchists and the Carlist supporters of the pretender would still be simmering a century later.

Up to 1873, there were no less than 12 military coup d'etats against an increasingly weak and corrupt government in Madrid, and in that year, on the abdication of Queen Isabella's well intentioned, but ineffectual, successor, the First Republic was proclaimed. This triggered another civil war and this Republic lasted only a few months. The monarchy (Alphonso XII) was restored under the political leadership of Canovas del Castillo, who devised a new constitution which effectively reasserted the power of the Church and the landowners – with a notionally elected parliament, the Cortez. Largely through corrupt electoral practices throughout every level of government, this constitution would last for the next 50 years.

Spain stayed neutral during WWI and did not suffer the deprivations of the main protagonists, but it was a very impoverished country. The population increased dramatically. The economy failed to grow in the 1920s, however, and then suffered from the fallout of the Wall Street Crash at the end of the decade. Unable to come to terms with the loss of its colonial Empire, the national psyche had an aimlessness that was in stark distinction to that of the other leading European nations. The bulk of the population were rural peasants who lived on the borderline of subsistence, while the lot of those who had migrated to the cities was if anything even worse.

The monarchy had survived – just. But in 1921 the army suffered a humiliating defeat in a battle against supposedly primitive tribesmen in the Rif mountains of Spanish Morocco. The King was blamed, and into the subsequent political vacuum stepped the first military dictator, General Primo de Rivera. He declared martial law, which stabilised the situation for a time, and he enjoyed an initial period of support from all facets of Spanish society. His instincts were patrician, but he was a sufficient realist to recognise that the Trade Unions had to be some way involved in Government and he appointed one union leader, Largo Caballero, as a councillor of state. Caballero's acceptance was seen as an act of treason by other union leaders, and instead of uniting the forces of Socialism, it precipitated a fragmentation that would later prove disastrous. Strikes in the industrial regions became more frequent, while in the countryside there were increasing pressures for agrarian reform.

Matters came to a head in 1931, when King Alphonso XVIII abdicated and the 2nd Republic was declared on February 14th. A coalition government from six different parties was formed under the presidency of Alcala Zamora, though historians were quick to point out parallels with the Kerensky government that followed the deposition of the Russian royal family in 1917. Spain was a tinderbox of social, economic and political instability and in the following years the tensions mounted, as the factions of the Left and the Right became increasingly polarised. It was only because of internal power struggles within both sides that the 2nd Republic lasted as long as it did.

On the Right were the Church, the aristocracy, the two monarchist parties and the Fascists (Falangists). Opposing them were the (moderate) Socialists, the academics and students, various Trade Unions, each with different agendas, and two quite distinct parties of the far left – the Communists and the Anarchists. Added to which was the further complication that two economically important regions of the country, Catalonia and the Basque region, were pushing once again for independence from rule by any Government in Madrid – as promised by a number of earlier administrations.

Somewhat distinct from these opposing factions (and in effect the only organisations with military hardware) were the armed services; or rather the Army and the Navy, because Spain had no airforce. The Navy had its headquarters in Malaga, but its units were dispersed around other ports both in the Mediterranean and on the Atlantic coast and it had never taken a political role. The Army in Metropolitan Spain was distributed among a number of city garrisons, consisting of untrained recruits and officers who were increasingly resentful at their lack of career prospects, poor pay and diminished status in Spanish society. But there was one substantial unit that had had battle experience, was relatively well funded and carried out a strict training programme, and that was the Army of North Africa. The troops were mainly locally recruited Moors. Remote from interference from Madrid, General Franco had convinced himself that the only way to restore Spain's national pride and unity was yet another military coup d'etat, with himself as saviour – the 'caudillo'. After a covert flight from 'exile' in the Canary Islands to Morocco, he had been able to hold secret negotiations with envoys from both Germany and Italy, who promised him tanks, aircraft and 'advisors'. If his coup was to be successful, he had to be able to rely on a simultaneous rising by all military garrisons on the mainland. By July 1936, most elements of his plan were in place, but although he was certain of support from Generals such as Quiepo de Llano in Seville, some other commanders – including, crucially, the commandant in Madrid – were still uncommitted. No one was certain where the loyalties of the civil guard (the paramilitary arm of the police) would lie. Spies from the Republican secret police were everywhere; priests were being murdered and churches torched; strikes became endemic. General Franco set a date for his rising, but it would only need one incident to detonate the tinderbox prematurely – and on July 12, an outspoken, right-wing firebrand called Jose Calvo Sotelo was assassinated in Madrid.....

With acknowledgements to Anthony Beevor; 'The Battle for Spain – The Spanish Civil War, 1936–39'. Weidenfeld & Nicolson, 2006.

HMS Shamrock in Gibraltar.

'HMS Shamrock'. The 'S' class destroyers had been built in 1918/9 and numbered 67 ships – the last destroyers built for the Royal Navy until 1926. They were 276 ft long, had 3 four-inch guns and 4 torpedo tubes. Steam turbines of 29,000 horsepower imparted a maximum speed of 36 knots. Displacement weight was 1,075 tons.

Beach party. Ian and Ruth Macnair in the foreground; Mabel Wilkinson, 'Ninny', is on the right.

*Commander Ian Macnair in 'full fig' for a banquet in honour of the President of the Spanish Republic, April 21, 1936.
Ruth and Ian Macnair 'off duty'.*

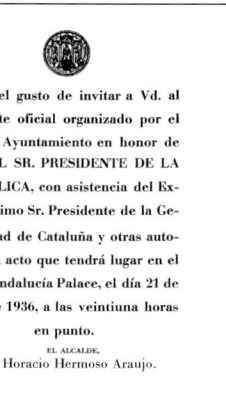
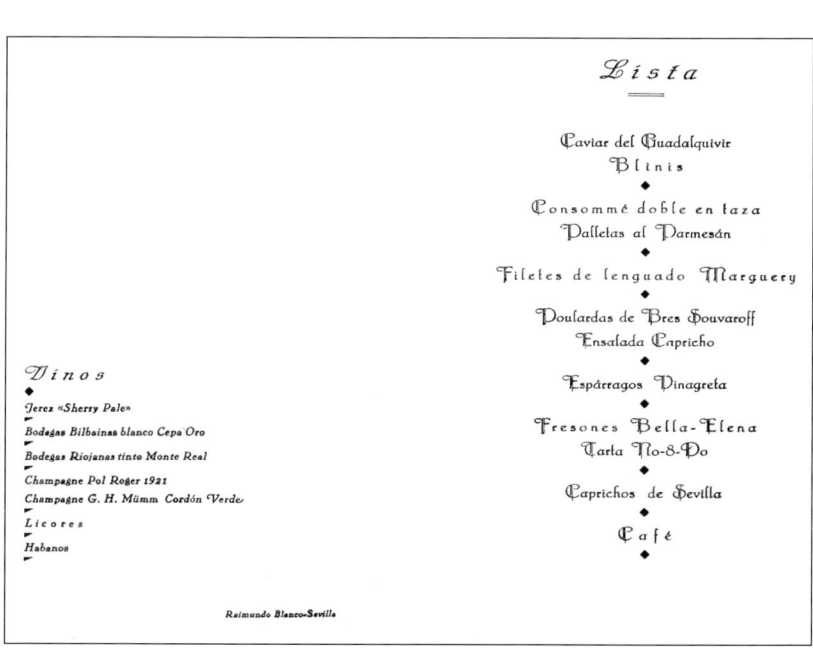

The banquet menu, April 21, 1936.

The Royal Calpe Hunt was an important part of the social life in Gibraltar between the wars, riding across the hinterland around La Linea and El Campemento. The scene might be anywhere in the English shires; apart from the palm tree.

The invitation to the launching of the RN Lighter by 'Mrs Admiral'. Ian and Ruth Macnair set off for the ceremony.

*Beach picnic, Easter 1936. Dionis, Ian and Eleanor Macnair –
on holiday from Downe House School. Eleanor went on to have a
distinguished career as an Admiralty scientist, designing propulsion systems
for the Royal Navy's experimental 'E class' submarines, powered by HTP.
She was awarded the OBE on her retirement.*

*Ian and Dionis Macnair. Dionis devoted her life to the New Forest,
its ponies and its unique traditions, becoming the first woman to be
elected as a Verderer.*

Ian Macnair with 'Miss Minx' in the Sierra Nevada, Spring 1936.

To get to the Sierra Nevada, this car ferry would have been used to cross the Guadiaro river near Sotogrande.

The frontier with Spain is most definitely closed, July 1936 – with barbed wire to make the point.

Ruth Macnair was on the jetty with her Brownie camera to record the disembarkation of the refugees from Seville, July 24, 1936. Ian Macnair is overseeing things, second from left.

HM Troopship 'Somersetshire' on which Ruth returned to England.

May Dent, Ruth's widowed mother, the recipient of the letters.

Witness To War

Sunday, July 20, 1936
24 Old Naval Hospital, Gibraltar

Darling mother,
We are living in stirring times here! Though in spite of being in the thick of it, I suspect that we probably know less of what is really happening than you do. But the place is full of wild rumours and tales. All communication with Spain by telephone etc. is cut and no news could be got of the English people in Malaga, so this morning 'Shamrock' was sent off there – with orders to get in touch with the Consul and either 'standby' or else return here with refugees. A whole party from here (the Dowes, Whitehouses, Vicarys, Wells-Coles and Buttershaws) had gone out to 'Owens' for the weekend, as on Saturday morning everything was perfectly peaceful and normal. A dockyard tug was sent to collect them and of course they had to leave their cars behind. Some of them had tried to get back by road, but a bridge near Estapona had been blown up, as well as being confronted by men armed to the teeth, who wouldn't let them through.

The first thing we heard was on Saturday night – that there had been a coup d'etat in Morocco and trouble was expected here and the frontier had been closed. On Sunday morning, while we were at church, we heard a bombardment (which rather distracted our concentration from the sermon!). A gunboat from Ceuta had come in and was shelling the barracks at La Linea, which was Communist. (The soldiers had seized and imprisoned their officers). Algeciras on the other hand was taken over peacefully by the 'Rebels' (who are largely Fascist) and we saw a transport from Morocco sail in to Algeciras harbour, where Foreign Legion troops were landed and proceeded to march to La Linea. In the evening, we went up the Rock with field-glasses, and at 7.30 there was a tremendous outbreak of firing. After about quarter of an hour we saw the garrison haul up a white flag, and this morning we heard that 150 had been killed in this little battle. The Foreign Legion are at present in possession, but Government (Communist) troops are reported to be coming from Malaga, so there is every likelihood of another battle. A Communist aeroplane arrived this morning and dropped bombs on Algeciras while we watched.

There is something most extraordinary in continuing to live one's normal life in safety in the very midst of all this! I took Di [1] to a birthday party at the Ellenburgers this afternoon. Major Ellenburger and Teddy de Brett came in looking very warlike. They are in charge of the Gate and another barrier with barbed wire has been erected further in, guarded by soldiers in tin helmets. The gate at Four Corners was nearly broken down this morning by huge crowds of refugees trying to seek sanctuary. The Marchesa Povar (who married one of the Larios family) has been badly wounded – Mr Elliot, the tailor, got a stray bullet in the hand. The Fulfords (Engineer Captain) had started on Saturday for Estoril in Portugal (everyone was celebrating the departure of the fleet by taking weekend leave!). They left here at 1 o'clock and not till they were nearly at Seville did they realise things were wrong. They found Seville deserted and all the hotels bolted and barred and the few people about walking with their arms up. Eventually, near the Plaza San Fernando, they saw a crowd and a Civil Guard, so they asked him what was the matter. He summoned a youth from the crowd, who spoke English, who said 'I am very sorry – but it is decided to have a revolution and it starts this afternoon.'

Then firing began. So they thought they had better come home, but they had a very trying journey, as they kept on being stopped by both soldiers and mobs and having the car searched. They had no food and arrived at La Linea at midnight almost done in, only to find the worst trouble of all right there! They nearly got shot and had an awful time getting back across the frontier.

We feel rather in a state of siege here – no fruit or vegetables or eggs or fish to be had. My poor old cook was in such a state that I have let her go to La Linea to see that her sister is alright. But I now hear that she probably won't be allowed back. I saw Mrs Hankey this morning, who was very worried at not being able to get any news of her sister, Mme de la Pasture, though later I saw the girl who makes gingerbreads and she said that Campemento was quite quiet and she had been able to get a pass to come into Gib. but only on foot.

The general opinion seems to be that it will be the only salvation of Spain if the military get control and set up a dictatorship. Things had become absolutely impossible under the present Government, but of course one doesn't know yet if the 'coup' has come off or not.

I shall be glad when Ian returns as I can't feel Malaga is a very healthy place at the moment. He took an RNR Lt. with him, who speaks Spanish, to act as interpreter.

I can hear heavy firing starting again just now.

It is sad to think that we probably shan't get into Spain again before I leave; I wonder if all this will delay 'Shamrock's' return?

I find all these happenings have a very unsettling effect – I haven't been able to do anything today, except gossip to everyone I meet and collect rumours! I think the 'Friendly Wife' picnic on Saturday will have to be cancelled, which is one blessing!

Your ever very loving Ruth.

[1] *Dionis was Ruth's second daughter, then aged 6.*

Monday, July 21
It is horrid getting no letters or papers, and I don't know how long it will be before you get my letters.

Events here are very dramatic – Ian went over to Ceuta today, but couldn't get in owing to a dense fog, and while he was waiting about in the Straits for it to lift, an aircraft came and bombed them (under the impression, of course, that they were a Spanish destroyer). Fortunately they didn't hit, but one bomb fell so close that Ian picked up pieces of shrapnel off the chart table! The 'Wild Swan', which was escorting the P&O liner was also bombed.

'Shamrock' got back last night from Malaga with 30 refugees. Commander Wavish kindly rang up and told me she was coming in at 9.30pm so I went down to the dockyard to see them arrive. Ian had his ensign flood-lit to try and prevent mistakes. They had had quite an exciting time at Malaga (and landing at Marbella to take off more refugees). Malaga is in flames and covered by a pall of smoke. All the villas, the Hotel Myrama and the entire main street are burnt. The British consul was quite calm – he told Ian he had spent most of his life in South America and so was used to it![1]

Today several Spanish Government ships arrived and anchored in the Bay (quite close in). They have declared a 'Soviet' and murdered or imprisoned their officers. They bombarded La Linea this afternoon and then aeroplanes came over from Morocco and bombed them, so they replied with anti-aircraft fire, some of the shells falling on the Upper Rock. We got a magnificent view from the tennis court and it was awfully exciting, though I couldn't believe it was real (especially looking down at Rosia, full of happy bathers!) Nobody seemed to score any hits, and now the warships have moved up to just off First River – I think under threats from us, as the bombing etc. was getting unpleasantly close.

On the way home from Sandy Bay, where I had taken Di as usual for a bathe, we came round by 4 Corners to look at the refugee camp. Just as I got to the gate, the car died on me! What an affront! And just at that moment the bombardment began, so Ninny [2] and Di got out and started to walk back by the Victoria Gardens.

Fortunately, with the help of some of the soldiers, I got the car going again. The whole place is full of refugees; I have rather rashly told the old cook she can bring her sister back here tomorrow as she is so worried about her. Nearly everyone has their maid's families parked on them, but the authorities are being stricter now and not allowing Spaniards in – only people born in Gibraltar – of whom a vast number live in La Linea, but of course are British subjects. La Linea itself is quite quiet, entirely in the hands of the 'Rebels' and with Moorish troops at every street corner.

The Gordon Highlanders are on their way back; much rejoicing from all their wives, so it's an ill wind.........

It is a most unsettling sort of existence; to go on with one's ordinary life seems like fiddling while Rome burns. Every time one hears a bang one rushes out to watch and the rest of the time you go round collecting rumours. In the morning you go down to the market early to try and get some of the few vegetables that are to be had – then to the Library to read the telegrams.

I feel I ought to be starting to pack. I don't know if I shall get passages in the 'Dempo' and if I don't, it will have to be the P&O on the 10th (which I am down for). I shan't regret leaving this place half so much now, but the trouble is I suppose that 'Shamrock' may be kept on. In the meantime, the sailors are enjoying it hugely and so I think is Ian – even the bombing! He has gone back to the ship now to see if there is any more doing; they expect to have a day off tomorrow, but it all depends on how things develop.

We are all hoping the Rebels will succeed, but it is touch and go. I hear the rebellion was not due to come off until the end of August, but the murder of that man in Madrid the other day precipitated matters. *(Jose Calvo Sotelo. MM)*. The navy going 'Red' has also been a setback.

I took Di to tea with the de Bretts yesterday and this evening I've been at the Dowses, so you see our lives go on more or less normally and we all have a lot to talk about. The weather is divine – hot today and not a breath of wind (which caused the tiresome fog in the Straits). We go every afternoon and bathe at Sandy Bay, but as two bombs were dropped there this evening, I fear it may be out of bounds now. The bathing picquet gave Di a row in their boat, which thrilled her; the soldiers told Ninny she was such a nice, polite little girl and she had such a pretty dress.

I enclose a bit of the local paper which will show you all the news we are getting. Poor Spain – such a lovely country!

PS. 'Shamrock' is not having a day off tomorrow after all. Ian has just come back to say they are off to Seville. A wireless message has just come through from the Consul asking for a ship to be sent. Rather interesting going right into the heart of the Rebel territory!

1 *The consul had advised that there were a bohemian Englishman and a young German Jew living 60 miles along the coast at the village of Almunecar, where a workers' militia had attacked the neighbouring village of Altofaro, which had been declared for the 'Rebels'. Ian Macnair took 'Shamrock' along the coast, anchored off the beach and launched a cutter to take them off. One of the pair was the poet Laurie Lee. In his autobiography, he described his leaving as follows; 'The King of England had sent a ship for the hotel fiddler and his friend, and our departure was a dramatic necessity..... The captain welcomed us with a handshake, like a squire at a picnic'.*

2 *Mabel Wilkinson, who had been nanny to Ruth Dent since birth and stayed with her to help bring up the children of the next generation. She weighed 20 stone and had a wonderfully comfortable, generous lap – I remember her with great affection. MM.*

Thursday, July 24
I am very relieved to have just heard that a wireless message has been received from 'Shamrock' to say she is clear of the river and on her way back with refugees. I expect Ian may have quite a lot of interesting things to tell, having been into the heart of the country held by the 'Rebels'.

I'm afraid things are as bad as they can be – there has been nothing like it since the Russian Revolution and it will be awful if Spain goes completely 'Red'; France will probably follow. So we can only hope that the 'Rebels' (which comprise Royalists, Fascists and moderates) will triumph, but it seems to be even chances at present.

Round here, all is quiet for the moment, the 'Rebels' having got control. Most of the locals (who aren't refugees here) have taken to the hills. I've got the old cook's sister living here; such a nice old thing, and she speaks French, having been in service in France. But she weeps a lot, being thoroughly unstrung, and the two poor old dears don't know what will happen to them when we go. I feel I ought to have one of the Owen children as I heard yesterday that they were all at the Grand Hotel with no money at all. However, I've been told that those kind Dugmores have taken two of them and the Pinks the nurse and the youngest child, so now I'm going along to tell Mrs Dugmore to let me take them off her hands sometimes and I will take them bathing etc.

I hope Ian will have a day off tomorrow. I've hardly seen him since the trouble started, but all the sailors and soldiers are rather enjoying it. Ian would have been very sick if he'd just gone home now that the 'Shamrock' is really being of use – especially as regards Seville – as they know their way about there and the consuls and pilots etc. 'Shamrock' is about the only thing with a shallow enough draught to get up there, so I don't expect she'll be coming home until things are either quiet enough or all the British are evacuated. I wonder what news of the Strangs? Barcelona sounds a nightmare – but they have 5 British ships there. Poor Mr Edwards and 2 other people started to motor home the day all this happened and haven't been heard of since.

Friday, July 25
We got a mail yesterday and English papers, the first for 6 days and I'm afraid any letters written during that time are lost for ever. But it was lovely hearing from you again, and from now on letters should come by sea alright.

We are all very annoyed with the English papers which are grossly inaccurate and also seem biased on the side of the Government (Republicans and Communists) while we are all hoping that the 'Rebels' will win, as this seems the only hope for Spain. If the Communists win, the reprisals will be so appalling and with Spain 'Red', France will follow suit in all probability and then what happens? It is all frightfully exciting and rather romantic – like the Stuart rebellion of '45.

Ian returned from Seville yesterday with 85 refugees (45 British including Mr Edwards who had been motoring home and got caught up in Seville. 20 Americans, a few French, and some Austrians). They had all their luggage – mountains of it! – especially the American tourists. One lady arrived clasping a large aspidistra! I saw them all disembark about 4 o'clock; the Admiral went to meet the ship and he and Ian walked up and down for half an hour talking. I took some photographs, which I will send you if they come out. On leaving, the Admiral said to me, 'Your husband has done very well.'

They had a most frightfully interesting time, but rather embarrassing as they got the most enthusiastic welcome and were greeted as being the first British ship to visit the new Government – which of course wasn't the case at all! They had only come to collect refugees and news. When the ship arrived at the mouth of the Guadalquiver, they were told that they couldn't get up as there was a boom across the river about halfway up, at a place where there were some villages controlled by the 'Reds'. The pilot didn't want to go, but Ian reckoned he could crash through a boom, though if he couldn't, it would be very awkward as the river is too narrow to turn round in! However, the boom had gone and the villages were displaying white flags. Also some aeroplanes appeared from Seville and escorted them up stream. Ian wasn't certain at first if they were friendly or otherwise, so he had the Lewis guns manned and protective mattresses put round the bridge etc.

On arrival at Seville, they were greeted by huge numbers of Fascists who cheered and clapped and gave them a most enthusiastic welcome. Ian was whisked off in a car with armed Fascists standing on the running-boards and taken to the headquarters of General Queipo de Llano. He had a very interesting interview with him and said he struck him as being a fine man. He (the General) said of course it meant death for them all if this revolt failed, but that he would prefer to be dead than live in Spain under the 'Reds' – and in effect controlled from Moscow. Ian lodged his protest about the bombing.

At 10pm, Maharada – Ian's Royalist friend – and his party all came on board and stayed till after midnight. They are all very pleased (Ian felt they were almost over confident) but he said the enthusiasm was most inspiring. The streets were all crowded with people and very little damage seemed to have been done. The cathedral was still intact. A shell had gone through the dining room of the Ingleterra Hotel and killed a waiter. 'Shamrock' sailed as soon as it was daylight and had an uneventful trip back.

Last night Gen. Franco landed troops at Algiceras and this morning at 6am we were wakened by planes bombing the place. Later the 3 battleships came from Malaga and bombarded Ceuta – but I think they kept out of range of each other and no shells were seen to hit. People watched it all from Europa Point – shells splashing all around – but by the time I got there, the ships were steaming away.

Last night we went to a dinner party at the Wavish's, with the Wells-Coles and Ellenburgers, and tonight we are going to the de Bretts. The 'Shamrock' is at 4 hours notice, but the Admiral said he probably wouldn't send her off again before Monday. I can hear aeroplanes now – I think they are the ones bringing troops over from Morocco to Algiceras. I took the Owen children off Mrs Dunmore's hands most of today – we bathed at Sandy bay and they and the Ellenburgers came back to tea. Doesn't it seem incredible to be leading one's normal life in safety in the very middle of naval, air and land battles!

The Gordon Highlanders arrived in HMS 'Repulse' this morning and she is staying here, so the Local Defense Flotilla is considerably strengthened! However, 'Shamrock' has had the most interesting jobs – first going to Malaga and seeing it in the hands of the 'Reds' and then to Seville, held by the opposing side; not to mention being bombed at Ceuta in the interval.

Heaps of love and excuse a disjointed letter, but there seems such a lot to say and I'm hurrying to catch the mail.

Wednesday, July 30
Ian is still away at Tangier. Yesterday a sudden and fierce 'levanter' got up and blew a hurricane for a short time and it poured with rain. I quite expected to see 'Shamrock' back, but

they must have been able to ride it out and this morning the skies are blue again, with the wind coming strongly from the south-west.

I believe Tangier is a very interesting place to be just now, on account of the Spanish Fleet being there, and it is they who constitute the menace which is preventing Franco bringing over all his Moorish troops. I had a long talk with the Brigadier yesterday and he seemed to think the 'Rebels' were doing well and will ultimately win, but it will be a long and bitter business. Huelva has definitely been captured, which means the 'Rebels' have consolidated all this part and they are nearly into Malaga. One can't believe a word of the Government broadcasts. The C-in-C (Med) arrives today, which is rather trying for Admiral Pipon, who has managed very well by himself!

I played bridge last night and won 3/9 pence. This morning I'm taking the children to see a new lighter that has been built in the dockyard and is going to be launched by Hermione Pipon. Tomorrow the KOYLIs are trooping the colour at 9am, so you see our life is wonderfully unchanged and even vegetables are obtainable now. Di is frightfully pleased at having Philippa Owen to stay and she is such a nice child. Mrs Vicary has got John and Mrs Pink has George and the nurse. I'm almost sorrier for the Owens than anyone – they had every penny sunk in their hotel at Malaga and even if it isn't burnt or looted, it is going to be a long time before people go to Spain for pleasure.

I enclose a letter I've had from that attractive Senora Abarzuza who we met at Ronda. Poor thing, it must be anxious for her with her husband at Cadiz, though he is probably fighting with the Fascists who are in control there. I still haven't made any plans for myself – it is difficult with Ian away and out of touch – but Commander Murphy thought he might be back tomorrow. I have started to pack a bit, but now I must hurry off to the market as things get sold early and, with 2 refugees, we are quite a large party to feed. I long to hear how Eleanor [1] is getting on in Scotland.

[1] *Her eldest daughter, then aged 15 and on holiday from Downe House school.*

Monday, August 3

I hope you won't be disappointed but I've definitely decided to stay here until the 16th and have booked passages in the Nederland Line boat the 'Johann de Witt', which leaves here at noon on the 16th and gets to Southampton on the 19th about 4pm. It is a smallish ship and they can't guarantee passages until the ship leaves Genoa. But failing that, there is a P&O on the 17th and I should get off at Plymouth on the 20th as Ian will be bringing most of the luggage.

The reasons for my staying are:

a) I don't think I could have got off by Friday; with Ian being away all last week, we were unable to make plans or get anything seen to (such as crates being repaired in the dockyard etc). Having the house full, all my linen was in use and Anna the washerwoman has had a poisoned hand – so Ninny's inevitable bugbear about the 'washing' loomed very large.

b) The 'Dempo' had only a small 2 berth cabin and they couldn't tell me until Tuesday whether they'd be able to give me the third passage, which would have been in a cabin with someone else. It is a very popular ship and always full.

c) Ian heard privately that HMS 'Vanoc' wouldn't be ready before August 25, so in the existing circumstances 'Shamrock' certainly won't be going home before the end of the month.

d) Another reason I'm rather ashamed to confess is that things are so interesting here that I feel I cannot bear to be 'out' of it at present!

Actually everything is quite peaceful all around here now – and most refugees have returned home. (My old lady left yesterday). I gather the country people are terrified of the Moorish troops; being totally ignorant and uneducated, they think it is another Moorish invasion of Spain. The buses have started running again to Seville and now that the 'Rebels' have taken Huelva, all this part of the country is in their hands and quite peaceful. The road to Malaga is still blocked from Estapona onwards, but a destroyer put in to 'Owens' and left them some tins of bully beef and reported that they were alright.

Ian had a pretty unpleasant time in Tangier in a very strong levanter; he was very relieved when on Friday evening he was suddenly recalled. The C-in-C (Med) had arrived and wanted him to attend a conference. Ian docked at 7 and the conference lasted all evening. The International situation is beginning to get a little difficult, with France sympathising with the Spanish Government and Italy and Germany with the 'Rebels'. Tangier is of course one of the most tricky places, being 'international' and the ships of all nations gathered there. France and Italy have sent cruisers, and even Portugal has sent 2 torpedo boats; there was something rather amusing about Great Britain being represented by little 'Shamrock'. However, we have now sent the 'Galatea', the ship which brought the C-in-C from Malta.

Did you see that questions were asked in the House of Commons about the 'Shamrock's' visit to Seville? (Thursday July 30). A socialist MP got up and demanded that disciplinary measures should be taken against the commanding officer for having paid a courtesy call on a rebel general. The Admiralty cabled to Ian for a statement and it is his reply that was given.[1]

The Admiral backed him up; there was no choice really in the matter as Ian had to go with the Consul to see the General about the removal of the refugees and it was not intended to be an official call on the new Government, which was how the General broadcasted it. Both sides have broadcast the most amazing amount of lies; but the Government even more than the 'Rebels'. It has completely shaken my faith in anything I read in the newspapers.

Laurie Lee wrote in his autobiography; 'About midnight, we got through to Radio Sevilla, and heard Queipo de Llano exulting in the fall of the city. The rebel general was drunk, and each slurred, belching phrase was a slap in the face of the militia. 'Christ had triumphed' he ranted, 'through God's army in Spain, of which Generalissimo Franco was the sainted leader. The criminal forces of socialism, which drew their slime across the country, were being routed by the soldiers of righteousness.'

We have had 3 days of pretty nasty levanter, but it has gone today and we hope to take a picnic lunch to Sandy Bay.

Yesterday we went to see the KOYLI 'troop the colour'; it was 'Minden Day' so all the soldiers wore white roses in their helmets. Apparently the KOSBs [2] do also, as they were one of the regiments that fought at Minden.

It seems strange somehow to be taking part in a ceremony like that, with real battles going on so close. I must stop and take the children to church.

[1] *Mr GALLACHER asked the First Lord of the Admiralty whether he had any information concerning the courtesy visit paid by HMS Shamrock to General Queipo de Llano, leader of the rebel forces in Seville last week, when that vessel put in at the port of Seville last week, and if he would cause such disciplinary action to be taken as would deter a repetition of such slights to a foreign power.*
SIR S. HOARE – It was necessary for the commanding officer of HMS Shamrock to call on the military officer in 'de facto' control of Seville in order to make arrangements for the evacuation of British subjects, and to lodge a protest concerning the bombing of British vessels. The call on General de Llano cannot be termed a courtesy visit, and the second part of the question does not arise. (Ministerial cheers).
MR GALLACHER – If no courtesy visit was paid by a British officer to Spanish officers, should a statement to that effect not have been made by the British authorities when the Press reports first appeared? (Ministerial cries of "Oh!")
SIR S. HOARE – The Hon. Member has himself given me the opportunity of making the necessary statement. (HANSARD).

[2] *The King's Own Scottish Borderers Regiment. Ruth's father – Edgar Dent (1863–1907) – had been a Captain in the regiment and had fought under Kitchener in the Sudan in 1889–90.*

Happier days. The 'Rock' seen from the hills behind Algeciras during a picnic earlier in 1936.

The bridge at 'First River'.

The Macnairs' married quarters in the Old Hospital.

A hill-top farm near Terifa.

El Campemento.

The Republican heavy cruiser, 'Jaime 1', shelling Algeciras, August 6, 1936.

Fishing boats on a beach.

The 'Rock', from near La Linea.

Dionis Macnair.

Still-life 1.

Still-life 2.

Fishing boats in Algeciras bay.

The editor. (Painted in England, 1937).

Wednesday, August 5
We hope that this week may bring some sort of resolution in Spain, though both sides seem so equal and so determined that I suppose it may drag on.

As far as 'Shamrock' is concerned, the ships are being withdrawn from Spanish ports now that most of the English people (and other foreigners) have been evacuated, and a cruiser has gone to Tangier as being more suitable to maintain the dignity of Great Britain than 'Shamrock'. So she is at the moment 'emergency destroyer' – that is to say she is at 2 hours notice and will be the one called to go if anything arises. Practically all the 'B' class destroyers are back in harbour from their various billets and C-in-C (Med) has departed on HMS 'Queen Elizabeth'. Ian lunched with him yesterday.

Ian had quite an interesting time in Tangier, meeting the captains of all the other foreign ships and attending a conference of COs at the Italian legation. (The Italian Consul is the 'doyen'). Coming back in the teeth of a levanter and going fast to be in time for the C-in-C's conference, they shipped 2 or 3 terrific seas and did themselves quite a bit of damage of a minor sort. So 'Shamrock' is looking rather disreputable at present – especially as she also blistered the paint off her funnels in the hurried dash to Malaga.

One of the other destroyers picked up an elderly English widow at some little port and then was ordered on to Alicante – so the lady remained on board for 5 days rather to the embarrassment of the officers; though it might have been worse if she had been young and beautiful!

The levanter is still blowing hard and is rather detestable – this is the first one we have had since April. Things are quiet here inland, but lots of excitement at sea. Every day there are encounters at sea between aeroplanes and warships in the Straits. This morning one of the Government destroyers was hit and rushed into the commercial harbour here, where I believe she has landed her wounded sailors. If she remains, she will of course be impounded; it is a difficult question for the authorities when the Spanish of both sides come here for sanctuary. In fact the whole international aspect bristles with difficulties and dangers! We saw the German pocket-battleship pass and go into Ceuta, where the 'Rebels' gave them a great welcome. Yesterday there was a lot of firing in the Straits and the P&O sailed out right into the middle of it!

Philippa Owen is still with me and very little trouble, but I'm finding it rather difficult to get another roof for her, as I shall have to turn her out next week when we really pack. People have either got their own children out for the holidays or else, if they haven't children of their own, they don't like taking one on.

The Dowses gave us a farewell dinner last night – the Vicarys also gave us one, but it was while Ian was away unfortunately. I wanted to have a farewell cocktail party on the tennis courts, but dare not arrange it in advance in case 'Shamrock' is at sea. We have been having some good tennis in the evenings lately. Life is really quite normal again now, but of course we talk and think of little else except the Revolution. I wish the 'Rebels' could get on a little faster – I'm afraid they are largely held up by these ships in the straits which prevent them bringing their Moorish troops across, and in spite of the theorists, aircraft don't seem to be able to do much against them (one up to Ack-ack!)

It will be enchanting to see you and Eleanor again; I'm so glad she did so well in her exams if not in her form. In this she follows her father's example – always among the top 3 or 4 in exams at Dartmouth but in the lower half of his term for form work. (I suppose this shows brains combined with laziness!). Ian should also be home by the end of the month – bringing 'Miss Minx'.[1] I shan't have nearly as many regrets at leaving as I would have had two months ago, and also nearly everyone we know will also be leaving soon.

[1] *Their Hillman car.*

Friday, August 7

I'm glad I wasn't leaving on the 'Dempo' this morning – we watched her going out at 9am, straight into a naval bombardment, with shells bursting all around her, some really close! The bombardment started at about 7.45 (when I was in my bath) and we rushed off to Europa Point to watch. It was the 'Jaime I', the big Government battleship and 2 modern cruisers and a destroyer. They were doing an intense shelling of Tarifa and Canera Point (where the lighthouse is just beyond the Sandy Bay at Algiceras). There was reported to be a field battery there, but I'm afraid it must have been knocked out. The 'Jaime I' steamed slowly in right up to Algiceras and proceeded to shell the town. It was rather awful seeing the flashes and explosions and then the boom, which set all our windows rattling. (They were 12 inch guns). The only comfort was to think that all the inhabitants had probably taken to the hills outside. Two shells burst near the Reina Christina Hotel but I don't think they actually hit it. They were really concentrating on the ships in the harbour and they succeeded in hitting an old torpedo boat at point blank range, which went up in clouds of flame and smoke.

We spent the morning sitting in the garden watching – and wishing there was something to reply as the 'Jaime' seemed to be having it entirely its own way. A big aeroplane did appear, but it dropped its 8 bombs outside the harbour, aiming at the destroyer – which it failed to hit, though 4 of them went very close. The destroyer and cruisers answered with pom-poms and anti-aircraft guns. About noon, all the ships packed up and departed in the direction of Malaga, leaving Algiceras covered in a pall of smoke. I (rather cold bloodedly) sat down and did a painting of it – not very good as it was very hazy, but I may send it up to one of the illustrated papers.

About 3 o'clock in the afternoon, the ships all reappeared and the 'Jaime' again steamed down opposite Algiceras and proceeded to plonk shells into the town. We were having tea with the Greeves (preparatory to playing tennis on the Gunners' court) so from the Royal Artillery mess we had a magnificent view. A man with a cine-camera was there taking film for the newsreels. The Brigadier was there too and I felt he was absolutely itching to loose off one of the Rock's big guns at the 'Jaime'. It was a most brutal and unjustifiable attack in the afternoon – the attack in the morning on the ships in the harbour was different as it had a clear military objective. Once again an aeroplane appeared but did no damage.

I forgot to tell you that on Wednesday evening, about 5.30, Franco got a convoy of troops and lorries over from Morocco; they were attacked on the way by 2 destroyers, but the poor old gunboat and an aeroplane kept them off. I had gone to fetch Ian, who was playing cricket on the North Front, and just as I arrived, one of the anti-aircraft shells had gone whistling over their heads and landed (and exploded) on the racecourse, where a game of polo was in progress. The ponies didn't mind a bit!

You can imagine how grateful we have been lately for your present of those very good field-glasses – which are in almost constant use. It is intensely interesting being in the midst of all this, but very heart-breaking to think of the future of Spain. As the Brigadier said this afternoon, they are probably shooting all the communist prisoners in Algiceras as a reprisal. I wonder what will happen tomorrow.

Sunday, August 9
Everything has been quiet here yesterday and today, except that the frontier has been completely closed so that no vegetables etc. can come in; there was almost a free fight for potatoes in the market. And the maids who went to La Linea for their day off have not been allowed to return, so many people are cookless! Even the men who work in the dockyard are not allowed in.

The C-in-C (Med) has also returned in HMS 'Queen Elizabeth' – I don't know if that portends anything. We spent a very happy, lazy day at Sandy Bay, taking our lunch and bathing both before and after. The water was lovely and warm, with big waves after the levanter. It was rather like Margate on a Bank Holiday, but as one knew everyone, it was rather fun. We shared a patch of shade with the Pipons and the Bradshaws. About 3 o'clock, Mr Ewing appeared saying a signal had arrived ordering the 'Shamrock' to 'proceed to sea' at 7.30, and I have just watched them sailing out – plastered with White Ensigns! I don't know on what mysterious errand they are bound, but they expect to return tomorrow.

I am very busy starting to 'turn out' preparatory to packing. I had my last dinner-party last night – it was a difficult day to get anything to eat except tinned stuff, of which there is fortunately no shortage. We had the Wavishes (who leave next week) Dudley and Jo Douse and the de Bretts (who go next month) and we went to an excellent film of the novel 'Jalna'.

In the morning I took Philippa to the Joneses who are having her for a visit while I pack – I also went to see Mrs Pipon, who was so nice and affectionate. There is something most lovable about her; so unselfish and simple. On picnics she always seems to be the one laden with baskets and buckets and rugs, so unlike the typical 'Mrs Admiral'. They have got the Cumberledge family at the Mount as their refugees – the baby is to be born there and may arrive any minute and, judging from her appearance, it is undoubtedly going to be twins.

I saw Mrs Smith from Algiceras yesterday. She said that a shell from the 'Jaime' landed in their garden and wrecked their cowman's house (fortunately no one in it). Half Algiceras was sheltering in their cellar! They say that surprisingly little damage was done, considering that several 12 inch shells were fired into the town at point blank range. All the cork on the jetty caught fire, which made a most imposing blaze.

I haven't yet heard if I've got passages on the 'Johann de Witt' – in some ways I hope it will be the 'Strathnaver' on the 17th, as I know so many people going in her and also it would be interesting to call in at Tangier. On the other hand, so much more convenient to arrive at Southampton. It won't be long now before we are re-united – that will be so exciting.

Not a word about the 'Shamrock's' return!

Monday, August 10

Don't expect much more in the letter line from me, because between packing and social engagements I don't see a spare moment ahead. I still haven't heard about passages, but Ian will cable you as soon as we leave with expected time of arrival etc.

Ian managed to get back late last night and we lunched on board HMS 'Galatea' today with Admiral 'D' – Somerville by name and very nice. I was the only female present. In the middle of lunch, Ian got a signal to say they were to go onto one hour's notice, which meant raising steam. Apparently the C-in-C wanted 'Shamrock' to reinforce the 'Queen Elizabeth' should there be firing in the Straits – which seemed probable as the Spanish ships were cruising about – and the idea was to keep merchant shipping out of the way while it was going on. However, nothing materialised, except for some machine-gunning from La Linea. Ian played cricket; a most exciting match against the KOYLIs which the Navy won with the last man in. We are lunching at 'The Mount' on Wednesday and with the Governor on Friday – plus farewell cocktail parties every evening.

Rumour has it that the ships in the hands of the 'Rebels' are coming down from the north to engage those belonging to the 'Reds' down here, in which case there will probably be *the* most spectacular battle in the Straits! It is so sad to think of the havoc in Spain.

Friday, August 14

I am undergoing agonies trying to make up my mind! I still can't get the Nederland line to say whether they can give me passages on Sunday and in the meantime I've been told there is an almost empty Trooper going to Southampton on the 25th – in which I am practically certain to be able to get 'indulgence' passages. This would save us over £10 and be First Class instead of Second. Also there seems no prospect of Ian coming home yet. In fact the Admiral said as much, so, as I can keep the flat on, I'm awfully tempted to stay until the 25th. On the other hand, I hate cabling you again to put off and also missing another 8 days of Eleanor's holidays – and her birthday.

Of course every week that Ian spends here now means another week on the other end before he goes to a new job. So I expect you will have quite enough of the family even if we don't arrive until the 29th. It will be very tiresome if he doesn't get his leave until October or November and can't get settled in his new posting, but I daresay he is doing more good in the 'Shamrock' at present – though there has been very little doing of interest this last week. Only 'alarms and excursions' – steam up in the middle of the night etc.

So on balance I think I will cable you to postpone, and I may get completely had if I don't after all get Trooper passages and have to come by the 'Ranchi' on Sunday or if Ian is whisked off to Huelva or somewhere next week. I'll leave it to the Nederland line to decide for me – whether they can get us a 3 berth cabin on Sunday or not.

Saturday, August 15
It has been decided for me – no room on the 'de Witt' tomorrow so I have taken the offer of the indulgence passages on the 'Somersetshire' on the 25th. The trooper is very slow and won't arrive in Southampton until the morning of Saturday the 29th,

but I only have to pay 32/6 for Di and myself First Class and £6 for Ninny. (They have lately put up the fares for nurses as so many people used to bring out un-entitled sisters or friends under the umbrella of 'nurses'!)

It is very tiresome there being no news about 'Shamrock's' returning to home waters – and as no captain has been appointed to the 'Vanoc', it means it must be a few weeks away. I must confess that I am pleased to have another week out here with Ian in the sunshine and warmth, but there is a chance he may be going to Huelva at the end of next week (in which case I would have to see myself off!). Ian wouldn't help me make up my mind about the passages at all, as he said that whichever course I decided to take, I should probably wish I'd taken the other! We are partially packed up and the house very dismantled and I've taken loads of clothes and books and toys etc. to jumble sales and refugee camps, but we still seem to have a lot of stuff.

Yesterday we lunched with H E at 'The Cottage' – such a nasty meal, with lumps of tough, grey mutton – but the Governor is always so nice and he was very interesting talking about the situation. In the evening, I gave a farewell cocktail party out on the tennis courts. About 70 people, a lovely sunset, a cool breeze and I think it was a success.

In the afternoon Ian was playing cricket and Di had gone off with the Wrights to tea on board the 'Java'. They bathed from the motor-boat in mid ocean. Neither Di nor Jill had brought any bathing costumes, so they just strapped canvas lifebelts around them and said they looked priceless with their little bare white behinds! Then (as Di described it) 'We went to the Yacht Club for drinks'. I asked her what she had and she answered 'Lemonade – I refused all the other things they offered me.' On Thursday she and the Mount children went to tea with Admiral Somerville on board HMS 'Galatea' and they all had a marvellous time; Di said 'I sat next to Flags at tea and he said the chocolate biscuits were foul and spitted his out – but I ate mine'.

Tomorrow Ian and I are dining on board HMS 'Queen Elizabeth' with the C-in-C. Everyone is feeling very hopeful that the 'Rebels' are going to win, though it is going to be a long and bitter struggle. They have been fighting all around the orange groves at Teserrillo and Buller's beach, but gained a definite victory and as they are close to Malaga on the Granada side, they hope to occupy Malaga, which would curtail the activities of the Govt. ships which have made it their base.

Such lovely weather! Warm, but not too hot. I have been rather touched to find how many people seem sorry to be saying goodbye to us – not necessarily the ones we were sorry to part with though!

Tuesday, August 18

The dinner party on board HMS 'Queen Elizabeth' last Sunday with the C-in-C produced the best meal I have had in Gibraltar. There has been no more local excitement, except for occasional firing in the Straits, but what is very interesting is that all over La Linea and San Roque we can see that they have hoisted the old Spanish colours (red/yellow/red instead of red/yellow/purple) and on Sunday, the Feast of the Assumption, religious services were held in La Linea and Algeciras and a procession at Seville, and apparently there was great popular enthusiasm. All the women wore their mantillas again.

From what we hear privately, I gather the 'insurgents' are making progress, and also we can prove that certain claims by the 'Government' are utter lies, like the recapture of Cadiz etc. The 'Shamrock' is at permanent 'short notice' and there have been one or two false alarms, but actually she hasn't been to sea for a week. They are expecting to go to Huelva shortly however.

Thursday, August 20
The C-in-C has signalled to the Admiralty requesting that 'Shamrock' should remain out here until the end of the crisis in Spain (which may be months) or until relieved by another destroyer (which will also take weeks). Rather trying. In the meantime, Ian has been whistled off to Tangier (needless to say there is another levanter!) and is then to go to Huelva and Cadiz to see that all is serene there. With luck they should get back on Sunday or Monday morning, just in time to see me off on Tuesday.

I have been able to fix up the poor old cook in a good job; also Anna the washerwoman. I've also had a commission to do a painting, which I am engaged on at the moment. It is rather a nasty day, with a wet cloud sitting over the Rock – which has thwarted Peggy de Brett and me from going sketching.

We dined with the Weilers yesterday. Mrs de la Pasture was there and it was awfully interesting hearing of her experiences in the first few weeks of the revolution out at Campemento, right in the thick of it, but pretty depressing, as although she says it is 'unthinkable' that the 'Reds' should win, she doesn't think it will be very much better if the 'Rebels' do! Which confirms my worst suspicions. But it will be very interesting to hear what Ian has to say after having been at Huelva (recently captured by the 'Rebels') and Cadiz, which the government claim to have recaptured – but haven't.

I can't say I am looking forward to 4 days in a trooper with Di and Ninny, but it will be convenient arriving at Southampton and lovely to see you and Eleanor again.

Saturday, 15 August
I've heard definitely that I have the passages in the 'Somersetshire' leaving here at 4 o'clock on Monday. I'm not sure exactly when we dock at Southampton – probably very early on Saturday morning, or else Friday night, but I'm afraid we may not be allowed ashore then. (On the 'Assaye', we lay off Netley all night). You will have to find out through the Transport Officer at Southampton.

Isn't it a blight? 'Shamrock' has been delayed at Tangier and won't get back here till Wednesday, so I will not see Ian again before we leave. Everyone is being very kind and helpful – we are all lunching with the Vicarys on Monday and a dockyard lorry is taking our luggage down. I am having supper with Peggy tomorrow and dining at 'The Mount' tonight, and as I've done most of my packing, I hope to do a last beach picnic tomorrow.

I'm really very sad at leaving and it is unsettling not knowing when Ian will return.

I won't write any more. With everything one hears about the revolution, the more appalling it sounds. Alas, poor, poor Spain.

Heaps of love,
Your ever, very loving Ruth.

Editor's postscript. By 1936, my mother had been told that she could not expect any more children. Her elder daughter, Eleanor, was 15, and her younger daughter, Dionis, 8 years younger. She had suffered numerous miscarriages in between. When Father came back from his dangerous, but thrilling, mission to Seville, he was understandably in a state of some excitement. I was born precisely 9 months later. MM.

HMS Shamrock.

Epilogue

"The British people should be proud of the work of the Royal Navy in these tense and dangerous times. By strict observance of neutrality, by courtesy and integrity, and by a humanity obvious to the most biased partisan, remarkable results were achieved."

The official histories of the Royal Navy make no mention of its involvement in the Spanish Civil War; that of WWI was still being written by the time WWII had broken out, and the latter conflict then occupied the historians' research efforts. It was left to a series of three articles in the 'Naval Review' (Volume LXII, 1974) by Peter Gretton to summarise some of the many activities in which the Navy was involved during the years 1936–39. The quotation above is taken from the first of these articles.

Even here, Ian Macnair's venture to Seville, a feat of considerable seamanship and diplomacy, is not mentioned. In the Public Record office there is the signal from the British Consul in Seville to the Foreign Office requesting assistance, followed up with a further cable to report that HMS Shamrock had departed on the morning of July 24, 1936, with an unknown number of refugees. 'Captain Macnair will doubtless prepare a manifest during his return to Gibraltar.' This, together with the report in Hansard and my mother's photograph, is virtually the only record that the incident ever occurred.

My father never had the ambition to strive for high office in the Royal Navy hierarchy; he was happiest just being in command of his own crew and his own ship, however small. He (and Mother) spent two years in Malta with another destroyer, HMS Verity, then back to Gibraltar in 1939, where he was in charge of the depot ship, HMS Cormorant. In 1941 he was offered the perfect command, a cruise liner, the 'Southern Prince', which had been converted into a Royal Navy mine layer based at Harwich. Unescorted, relying solely on their considerable speed, for eighteen months Ian Macnair raced back and forth across the North Sea, laying minefields around the German coast. Tragedy finally came when the ship was terminally disabled, not by a torpedo, but by one of its overstressed diesel engines blowing itself to pieces, leaving them a sitting target for several hours until rescued by a tug.

A period on the staff at HMS Vernon in Portsmouth followed and I still remember with childish glee my rare visits, being given brown sugar sandwiches by a charming WRNS orderly. In preparation for D-day in June 1944, my father was posted as Flag Captain to the Admiral in charge of the naval bombardment off the landing beaches, his vessel being a commandeered Southern Railway ferry, the 'Isle of Sark'. It was one of the smallest ocean going ships in the Navy and, by a neat irony, his final sea-going command was to be one of the biggest – the submarine/destroyer depot ship HMS Tyne. This vast whale of a ship he took out to Burma in 1945, where he was appointed C-in-C Akyab.

He ended his career as commandant of HMS King Arthur, the Petty Officer training establishment at Corsham, near Bath. He and Mother would enjoy his retirement for another 32 years, during which time he devoted himself to the Sea Cadets, the garden, writing poems for 'Country Life' and rebuilding their beloved golf course at Burley in the New Forest. He died on March 10, 1980.

"Home is the sailor, home from sea,
And the hunter home from the hill."